Jennifer Guerrero
the not so starving artist

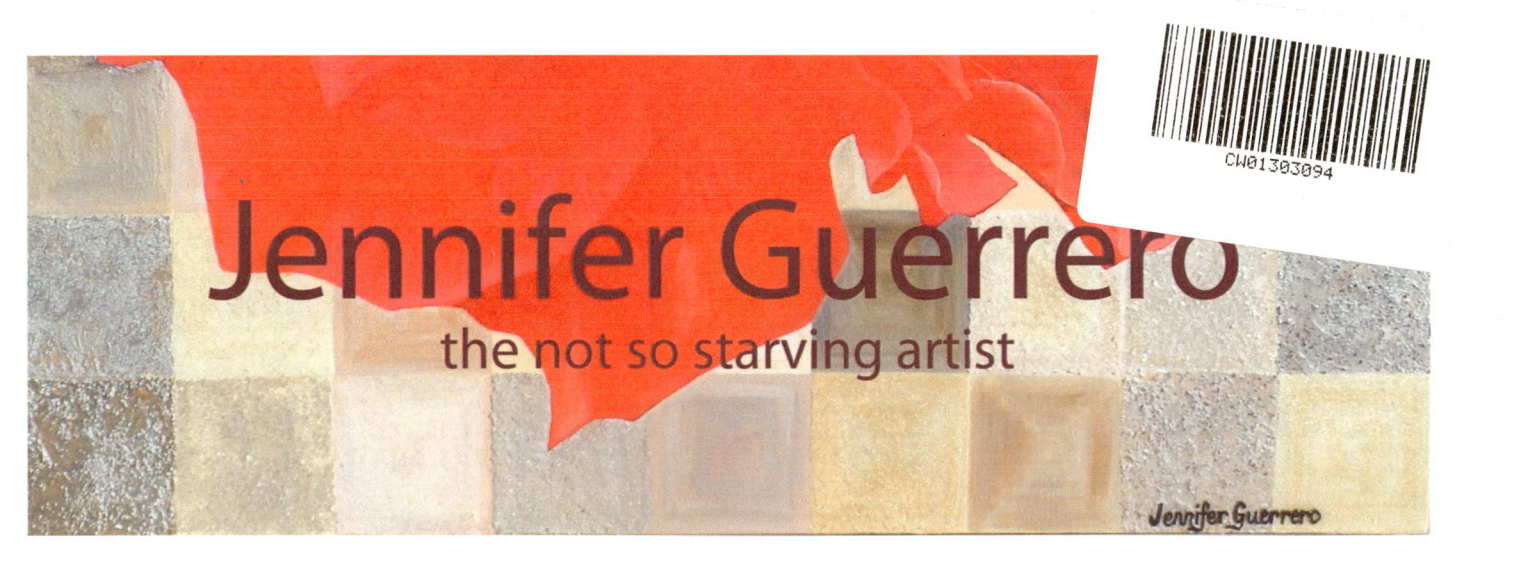

Jen's Protein Nice Creams,
Unofficial guide to high-protein ice creams in the Ninja Creami™ Deluxe
Copyright © 2024 by Jennifer Guerrero
www.JenniferGuerrero.com

Photo Credits: All photography in this book was taken by Jennifer Guerrero.

All rights reserved. No part of this publication may be reproduced, distributed, or transmitted in any form or by any means, including photocopying, recording, or other electronic or mechanical methods, without the prior written permission of the author, except in the case of brief quotations embodied in critical reviews and certain other non-commercial uses permitted by copyright law.

Jen's Protein Nice Creams

	Protein	Fat	Carbs	Calories	Page
Wild Blueberry	37	4	32	280	10
Lemon	38	5	51	239	11
Lemon decked out like pie	39	9	63	334	
Banana Berry	41	5	31	321	12
Strawberry	37	4	26	250	13
Strawberry shortcake	39	10	43	391	
Strawberry Daiquiri *(NO ALCOHOL!)*	37	4	43	266	15
Apple Pie à la Mode	37	4	55	358	16
Pineapple	37	4	35	315	17
Pina Colada *(NO ALCOHOL!)*	37	8	32	335	18
Mandarin Creamsicle	37	4	33	315	19
Chocolate Covered Orange	39	5	40	298	20
Peaches and Cream	38	4	36	270	21
Peach Melba	38	5	31	271	22
Jen's Apricot Cardamom Dreams	40	14	57	453	23
Pumpkin Pie à la Mode	38	5	40	266	24
Bananas Foster	38	5	54	319	25
Banana Chocolate Chip Walnut	47	19	61	566	26
Baby Guava	41	5	36	308	27
Chocolate Cherry	38	5	38	285	28
Cookies and Cream	39	12	41	413	29
Chocolate Malt	39	7	41	327	30
Chocolate Malt w/candy	39	11	59	435	
Chocolate Peanut Butter	50	9	40	358	31
Chocolate Peanut Butter w/candy	53	16	55	488	
Red Velvet	40	9	30	305	32
S'mores	40	12	59	440	33
Pistachio	44	19	24	395	34
King Cake	38	6	34	230	35
Churro	38	6	28	229	36
Cookie Dough	39	16	30	376	37-38
Thin Mint	35	12	43	413	39
Caramel DeLite	33	19	32	424	40
Biscoff	40	17	41	464	41

Thank you so much for picking up a copy of my book! I've given all my attention to creating protein-filled ice cream that tastes decadent and delicious. Boom. The flavors and textures are perfect. These would make any foodie smile. I am obsessed! I'm super excited to share them with all of you! Hope you love them, too!

xx Jen

Okay! You've memorized the instruction manual and you're ready to go!

Things that might help....

Texture: All the creamis in this book are cottage cheese and protein powder based. "Light ice cream" will give you something between soft serve and a smoothie bowl. It requires less re-spins. An insulated cup will help it from melting quickly. I use this setting whenever I want soft serve in an insulated cup. "Ice cream" gives a firmer texture. I use this whenever I want a bowl of firm scoopable ice cream.

ICE CREAM	LITE ICE CREAM
Designed for traditionally indulgent recipes. Great for turning dairy and dairy-alternative recipes into thick, creamy, and scoopable ice creams.	Designed for health-conscious consumers to make ice creams that are low in sugar or fat or use sugar substitutes. Choose when processing keto, paleo, or vegan recipes.

Salt: Adding a pinch of salt to desserts to enhance flavor is all the rage. No need to do that here! Cottage cheese is a little salty, and will take case of that enhancement for you.

Flavor: I am a massive flavorist. I made notes on some of the recipes about how important—or not—the mix-ins are to the flavor so that you can make the right decision for you!

Size: All of my recipes fill a 24 ounce Deluxe Creami container. If you have a Ninja Creami with 16 ounce containers, you'll just do 2/3 of each recipe. OR double the recipe and fill (3) 16-ounce containers.

Must have...

A Ninja Creami ice cream maker. Everything in this book is made for the Ninja Creami Deluxe, the 24 oz size. If you have a smaller 16 oz Ninja Creami, you'll have to scale the recipes to 2/3.

Nice to have...

An immersion (stick) blender. This is a lazy human's dream. Just insert it right into your Creami container and blend away. Yes, you could totally do this with a food processor, but this is much more streamlined and easier to clean up. I wouldn't recommend a hand mixer and bowl. It has a terrible time blending up the cottage cheese nicely.

Wine glass covers. When you put your blended base into the freezer for 24 hours, and pull it out, lots of times there's a weird frozen hump coming out of it like a little alien. What happened? Things expand when they freeze. We don't want that weird frozen growth to break our blade! What to do? Some people take a knife and shave it down. Others swear by leaving the container cover off til it's fully frozen. I like to pop a wine glass cover right on top of the mixture and then add the cover.

Everyone has personal preferences about ingredients. I have very intentionally included the protein, fat, carbs, and calories by ingredient so that you can easily swap in for your own preferences.

Ingredients I'm using....

Cottage cheese—Daisy 2%

Protein Powders
Optimum Nutrition vanilla ice cream
Optimum Nutrition extreme milk chocolate
Optimum Nutrition s'mores
GNC Thin Mint
GNC Caramel Coconut

Swerve
Regular
Brown Sugar
Confectioners

Extracts
Vanilla
Almond
Rum
Butter
Strawberry
Raspberry
Peach flavor
Buttery Sweet Dough Emulsion
Boiled cider

Boatloads of frozen fruit, nuts, unsweetened cocoa powder, mini chocolate chips, coconut, some cookies and candies, a sugar free Jell-o…..

Substitutions

<u>Milk</u> Can you use a different milk than almond milk? Absolutely!!! I love the flavor of almond milk, but definitely use your family's favorite milk!

<u>Cottage Cheese</u> Can you sub in anything for cottage cheese? Yes! Tofu! Tofu ranges from silky to firm. The silky has a milder flavor and less protein. The flavor is more pronounced in extra firm, but it has much higher protein counts....

I subbed in **half a block of well-drained firm tofu** for cottage cheese. I tried it on blueberry and strawberry. You could detect it in the blueberry, but it wasn't screaming for attention. It worked perfectly in the strawberry! None of us would have a preference between the cottage cheese and to-fruity strawberry! They did require extra sweetener, though - 1 extra Tablespoon in the blueberry and 2 in the strawberry, and a little extra almond milk in the re-spin. I tested fruit because the chocolate would definitely cover it.

LITE ICE CREAM

Designed for health-conscious consumers to make ice creams that are low in sugar or fat or use sugar substitutes. Choose when processing keto, paleo, or vegan recipes.

Tofu Cottage Cheese difference				
Daisy 2% cottage cheese 1 cup	26	5	10	180
Firm Tofu 8 oz	19	11	5	187
Tofu difference (whole 24 ounce container)	-7	6	-5	7

For half of a container...	Protein	Fat	Carbs	Calories
Wild Blueberry	37	4	32	280
Wild Blueberry - tofu	33	7	29	283

For half of a container...	Protein	Fat	Carbs	Calories
Strawberry	37	4	26	250
Strawberry - tofu	33	7	23	253

Overall.... For half of a container...

Tofu 4 grams **protein** less

Tofu 3 grams **fat** more

Tofu 3 grams **carbs** less

Tofu 3 **calories** more

If you are new to tofu, cut it into cubes, wrap it in a bunch of paper towel, put a heavy pot on it, and let it drain for 15 minutes. Ready to use!

You blended it! If it looks super creamy, you're ready. It looks crumbly? That is totally normal. Add 1-2 Tablespoons of Almond milk and hit "full" "re-spin".

Re-spin?

Ready for mix-ins? Awesome! Sometimes the machine leaves a well right up the center of the creami. If not, make one! Make your column as evenly as you can from the very bottom to the top so the goodies will get distributed evenly. Chop up those goodies!

They don't all fit???? Overflow are just toppings!

Press "full" and mix-ins".

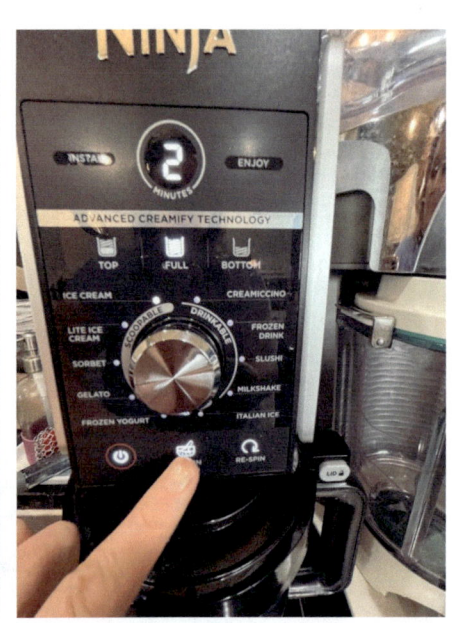

Mix-ins

Anatomy of a Mix-In

Does the order you add the mix-ins in matter? Totally! When you press that mix-in button, the blade spins and distributes the mix-ins at the same height they're at in the container.

If you drop chopped up frozen raspberries in the bottom half and mini chocolate chips in the top, the bottom half will be filled with little raspberry chunks and the top will be polka-dotted with chocolate chips. Cool if two people strongly disagree about what the mix-in should be.

If you mix up your mix-ins before you drop them in, the whole container will get little pops of raspberries and chocolate. Basically nirvana.

Wild Blueberry

Ingredient	Protein	Fat	Carbs	Calories
1 cup 2% Daisy cottage cheese	26	5	10	180
2 scoops vanilla protein powder (Optimum Nutrition Whey)	48	3	8	240
1 3/4 cups frozen blueberries, thawed (Wyman's wild)	0	0	33	140
1 Tablespoon Swerve	0	0	12	0
1 teaspoon vanilla extract				
Total	74	8	63	560
Half of that big old 24 oz Deluxe container	37	4	32	280

1. Measure all the base ingredients into your Creami container, making sure not to pass the max fill line.
2. Blend with your immersion (stick) blender til smooth and luscious.
3. Pop into your freezer for 24 hours.
4. Pop into your Ninja Creami Deluxe. Select full, make your selection, and hit the go button.
5. Take a peek. Perfectly creamy? Great! If not, add 1-2 Tablespoons of vanilla almond milk and select full and push the re-spin button. (Usually requires a re-spin.
6. Enjoy!

Measure frozen fruit while it's frozen!!!

Tastes like a vacation in Maine! :D More blueberries make a cute mix-in!

Makes a 24 oz Deluxe pint. Have a smaller 16 oz model? Cut all the ingredients to 2/3.

Lemon

Ingredient	Protein	Fat	Carbs	Calories
1 cup 2% Daisy cottage cheese	26	5	10	180
2 scoops vanilla protein powder (Optimum Nutrition Whey)	48	3	8	240
6 Tablespoons fresh squeezed lemon juice (about 3 lemons)	0	0	10	31
zest of 1 lemon	0	0	1	3
6 Tablespoons swerve	0	0	72	0
3/4 c vanilla almond milk	1	2	1	23
Total	75	10	102	477
Half of that big old 24 oz Deluxe container	38	5	51	239

Decked out Lemon - Half plus.....

Ingredient	Protein	Fat	Carbs	Calories
1/4 cup extra creamy Reddi wip	0	2	0	30
1 honey maid graham cracker sheet	1	2	12	65
Decked out Lemon Total	39	9	63	334

1. Measure all the base ingredients (not mix-ins or toppings!) into your Creami container, making sure not to pass the max fill line.
2. Blend with your immersion (stick) blender til smooth and luscious.
3. Pop into your freezer for 24 hours.
4. Pop into your Ninja Creami Deluxe. Select full, make your selection, and hit the go button.
5. Take a peek. Perfectly creamy? Great! If not, add 1-2 Tablespoons of vanilla almond milk and select full and push the re-spin button. (Usually requires a re-spin.
6. Enjoy!

Fresh raspberries would play fabulously with this, too!

Banana Berry

	Protein	Fat	Carbs	Calories
1 cup 2% Daisy cottage cheese	26	5	10	180
2 scoops vanilla protein powder (Optimum Nutrition Whey)	48	3	8	240
1 banana	1	0	27	105
1 c mixed berries	2	0	16	70
1 Tablespoon sugar free strawberry Jell-o powder *dissolved in a smidge of hot water*	4	0	0	40
1/4 c Vanilla almond milk *(to line - depends on banana size)*	0	1	0	8
Total	81	9	61	643
Half of that big old 24 oz Deluxe container	**41**	**5**	**31**	**321**

Opt: berries, granola, whipped cream

We preferred the Tablespoon of Jell-O here, but use this substitution if that's not your jam!!

1 Tablespoon Swerve	0	0	12	0
1 teaspoon strawberry extract				

Pile me on more bananas with sauce and whipped cream, sprinkles and a cherry on top if you're feeling it!

1. Measure all the base ingredients (not mix-ins or toppings!) into your Creami container, making sure not to pass the max fill line.
2. Blend with your immersion (stick) blender til smooth and luscious.
3. Pop into your freezer for 24 hours.
4. Pop into your Ninja Creami Deluxe. Select full, make your selection, and hit the go button.
5. Take a peek. Perfectly creamy? Great! If not, add 1-2 Tablespoons of vanilla almond milk and select full and push the re-spin button. (Usually requires a re-spin.
6. Enjoy!

Measure frozen fruit while it's frozen!!!

Makes a 24 oz Deluxe pint. Have a smaller 16 oz model? Cut all the ingredients to 2/3.

Strawberry 1

	Protein	Fat	Carbs	Calories
1 cup 2% Daisy cottage cheese	26	5	10	180
2 scoops vanilla protein powder (Optimum Nutrition Whey)	48	3	8	240
1 3/4 cups frozen strawberries, thawed	0	0	21	79
1 Tablespoon Swerve	0	0	12	0
1 teaspoon strawberry extract				
Total	**74**	**8**	**51**	**499**
Half of that big old 24 oz Deluxe container	**37**	**4**	**26**	**250**

Strawberry Shortcake – Half plus…

	Protein	Fat	Carbs	Calories
1 butter tastin Pillsbury biscuit	2	4	15	100
1/4 cup extra creamy Reddi wip	0	2	0	30
1/4 cup strawberries	0	0	3	11
Total, all dressed up for the party	**39**	**10**	**43**	**391**

Measure frozen fruit while it's frozen!!!

1. Measure all the base ingredients (not mix-ins or toppings!) into your Creami container, making sure not to pass the max fill line.
2. Blend with your immersion (stick) blender til smooth and luscious.
3. Pop into your freezer for 24 hours.
4. Pop into your Ninja Creami Deluxe. Select full, make your selection, and hit the go button.
5. Take a peek. Perfectly creamy? Great! If not, add 1-2 Tablespoons of vanilla almond milk and select full and push the re-spin button. (Usually requires a re-spin.
6. Enjoy!

Makes a 24 oz Deluxe pint. Have a smaller 16 oz model? Cut all the ingredients to 2/3.

Strawberry 2

	Protein	Fat	Carbs	Calories
1 cup 2% Daisy cottage cheese	26	5	10	180
2 scoops vanilla protein powder (Optimum Nutrition Whey)	48	3	8	240
1 3/4 cups frozen strawberries, thawed	0	0	21	79
1 Tablespoon sugar free strawberry Jell-o powder dissolved in a smidge of hot water	4	0	0	40
Total	78	8	39	539
Half of that big old 24 oz Deluxe container	39	4	20	270

Strawberry Shortcake 2 - Half plus...

	Protein	Fat	Carbs	Calories
1 butter tastin Pillsbury biscuit	2	4	15	100
1/4 cup extra creamy Reddi wip	0	2	0	30
1/4 cup strawberries	0	0	3	11
Total, all dressed up for the party	41	10	37	411

Two different strawberry recipes? Yes. I would pick differently for different occasions, and you might have an ingredient preference. They are super similar. Both get most of their strawberry flavor from a ton of strawberries. But, to get across the finish line....

*__Strawberry 1__ uses a small amount of strawberry extract and sweetener. It's really clean strong natural strawberry flavor.

*__Strawberry 2__ uses a small amount of sugar free strawberry Jell-O powder. It's a little sweeter and super pink.

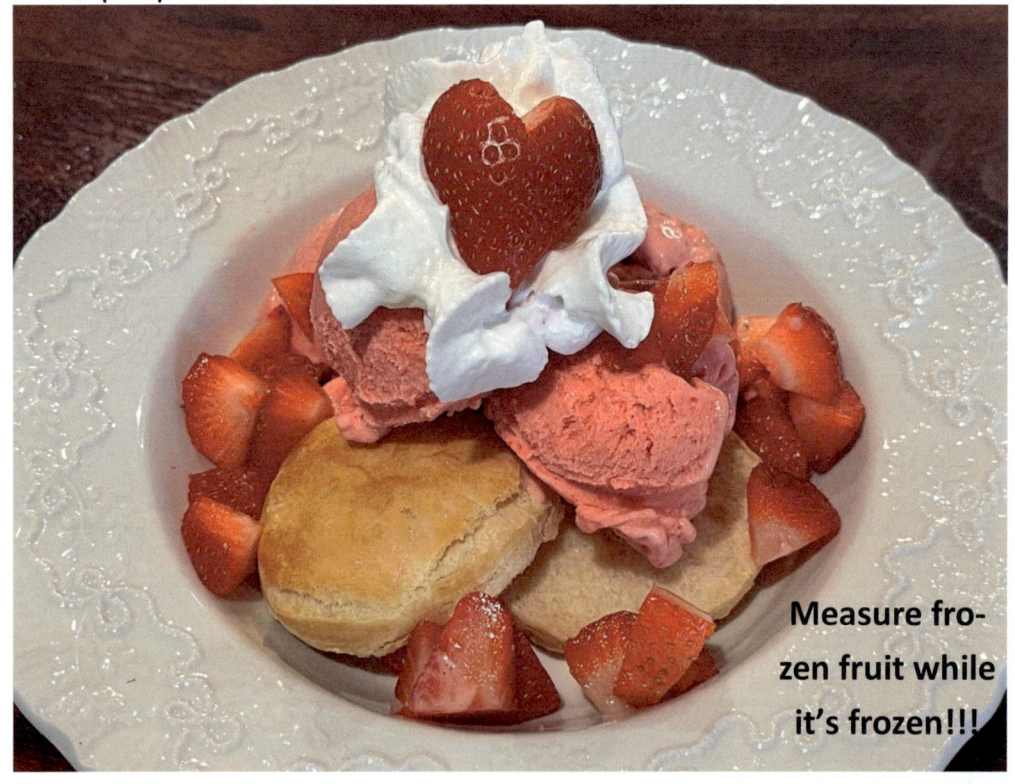

1. Measure all the base ingredients (not mix-ins or toppings!) into your Creami container, making sure not to pass the max fill line.
2. Blend with your immersion (stick) blender til smooth and luscious.
3. Pop into your freezer for 24 hours.
4. Pop into your Ninja Creami Deluxe. Select full, make your selection, and hit the go button.
5. Take a peek. Perfectly creamy? Great! If not, add 1-2 Tablespoons of vanilla almond milk and select full and push the re-spin button. (Usually requires a re-spin.
6. Enjoy!

Measure frozen fruit while it's frozen!!!

Makes a 24 oz Deluxe pint. Have a smaller 16 oz model? Cut all the ingredients to 2/3.

Strawberry Daiquiri

Ingredient	Protein	Fat	Carbs	Calories
1 cup 2% Daisy cottage cheese	26	5	10	180
2 scoops vanilla protein powder (Optimum Nutrition Whey)	48	3	8	240
2 cups frozen strawberries, thawed	0	0	24	90
zest of 1/2 a lime	0	0	0	1
juice of 2 limes	0	0	7	20
3 Tablespoons Swerve	0	0	36	0
1 teaspoon strawberry extract				
1 teaspoon rum extract				
Total	74	8	85	531
Half of that big old 24 oz Deluxe container	37	4	43	266

Measure frozen fruit while it's frozen!!!

Chopped up frozen strawberries make the cutest mix-in!

1. Measure all the base ingredients into your Creami container, making sure not to pass the max fill line.
2. Blend with your immersion (stick) blender til smooth and luscious.
3. Pop into your freezer for 24 hours.
4. Pop into your Ninja Creami Deluxe. Select full, make your selection, and hit the go button.
5. Take a peek. Perfectly creamy? Great! If not, add 1-2 Tablespoons of vanilla almond milk and select full and push the re-spin button. (Usually requires a re-spin.
6. Enjoy!

Makes a 24 oz Deluxe pint. Have a smaller 16 oz model? Cut all the ingredients to 2/3.

Apple pie à la Mode

Ingredient	Protein	Fat	Carbs	Calories
1 cup 2% Daisy cottage cheese	26	5	10	180
2 scoops vanilla protein powder (Optimum Nutrition Whey)	48	3	8	240
1 3/4 cups unsweetened apple sauce (Motts)	0	0	49	175
1 Tablespoon Swerve	0	0	12	0
2T boiled apple cider (optional, but fab flavor kick!) (Boiled cider is cider reduced to 1/8th. If you want to make it yourself, simmer 1 cup of apple cider down to 2 Tablespoons. Be sure to keep an eye on it!)	0	0	30	120
1 teaspoon lemon juice	0	0	1	2
1/2 teaspoon ground cinnamon				
1/8 teaspoon ground nutmeg				
1/8 teaspoon ground allspice				
1 teaspoon vanilla extract				
Total	74	8	110	717
Half of that big old 24 oz Deluxe container	37	4	55	358

Optional topping: fresh apples and pie crust pieces

There's no nutrition label on the boiled cider, so I had to go with my best estimate!

2 T boiled cider = 1 cup of apple cider

So I filled in the nutrition info from 1 cup apple cider.

1. Measure all the base ingredients (not mix-ins or toppings!) into your Creami container, making sure not to pass the max fill line.
2. Blend with your immersion (stick) blender til smooth and luscious.
3. Pop into your freezer for 24 hours.
4. Pop into your Ninja Creami Deluxe. Select full, make your selection, and hit the go button.
5. Take a peek. Perfectly creamy? Great! If not, add 1-2 Tablespoons of vanilla almond milk and select full and push the re-spin button. (Usually requires a re-spin.
6. Enjoy!

Makes a 24 oz Deluxe pint. Have a smaller 16 oz model? Cut all the ingredients to 2/3.

Pineapple

	Protein	Fat	Carbs	Calories
1 cup 2% Daisy cottage cheese	26	5	10	180
2 scoops vanilla protein powder (Optimum Nutrition Whey)	48	3	8	240
1 1/2 c crushed pineapple in juice	0	0	51	210
1 teaspoon vanilla extract				
Total	74	8	69	630
Half of that big old 24 oz Deluxe container	**37**	**4**	**35**	**315**

Makes a 24 oz Deluxe pint. Have a smaller 16 oz model? Cut all the ingredients to 2/3.

Feeling extra?? Turn it into a float with pineapple juice and a posh umbrella straw. Turn it into a sundae with coconut flakes, macadamia nuts, and more fresh pineapple on pound cake. Or just a smidge of whipped cream and a cherry for a wink and a nod at pineapple upside down cake.

1. Measure all the base ingredients (not mix-ins or toppings!) into your Creami container, making sure not to pass the max fill line.
2. Blend with your immersion (stick) blender til smooth and luscious.
3. Pop into your freezer for 24 hours.
4. Pop into your Ninja Creami Deluxe. Select full, make your selection, and hit the go button.
5. Take a peek. Perfectly creamy? Great! If not, add 1-2 Tablespoons of vanilla almond milk and select full and push the re-spin button. (Usually requires a re-spin.
6. Enjoy!

Pina Colada

	Protein	Fat	Carbs	Calories
1 cup 2% Daisy cottage cheese	26	5	10	180
2 scoops vanilla protein powder (Optimum Nutrition Whey)	48	3	8	240
1 1/4 crushed pineapple in juice	0	0	43	175
1/2 cup lite coconut milk	0	8	3	75
1 teaspoon rum extract				
Total	74	16	64	670
Half of that big old 24 oz Deluxe container	**37**	**8**	**32**	**335**

1. Measure all the base ingredients (not mix-ins or toppings!) into your Creami container, making sure not to pass the max fill line.
2. Blend with your immersion (stick) blender til smooth and luscious.
3. Pop into your freezer for 24 hours.
4. Pop into your Ninja Creami Deluxe. Select full, make your selection, and hit the go button.
5. Take a peek. Perfectly creamy? Great! If not, add 1-2 Tablespoons of vanilla almond milk and select full and push the re-spin button. (Usually requires a re-spin.
6. Enjoy!

Makes a 24 oz Deluxe pint. Have a smaller 16 oz model? Cut all the ingredients to 2/3.

Mandarin Creamsicle

	Protein	Fat	Carbs	Calories
1 cup 2% Daisy cottage cheese	26	5	10	180
2 scoops vanilla protein powder (Optimum Nutrition Whey)	48	3	8	240
3 containers mandarin oranges in juice	0	0	48	210
1 teaspoon vanilla extract				
Total	74	8	66	630
Half of that big old 24 oz Deluxe container	**37**	**4**	**33**	**315**

Need cream on that creamsicle? Half plus….

1/4 cup extra creamy Reddi wip	0	2	0	30
Creamsicle with extra cream	37	6	33	345

Make it a float with orange or pineapple juice. Pop it on pound cake with fresh oranges and coconut. Use chocolate Magic Shell for a chocolate covered orange. Drizzle it with caramel sauce for oh-la-la …

1. Measure all the base ingredients (not mix-ins or toppings!) into your Creami container, making sure not to pass the max fill line.
2. Blend with your immersion (stick) blender til smooth and luscious.
3. Pop into your freezer for 24 hours.
4. Pop into your Ninja Creami Deluxe. Select full, make your selection, and hit the go button.
5. Take a peek. Perfectly creamy? Great! If not, add 1-2 Tablespoons of vanilla almond milk and select full and push the re-spin button. (Usually requires a re-spin.
6. Enjoy!

Makes a 24 oz Deluxe pint. Have a smaller 16 oz model? Cut all the ingredients to 2/3.

Chocolate Covered Oranges

Ingredient	Protein	Fat	Carbs	Calories
1 cup 2% Daisy cottage cheese	26	5	10	180
2 scoops chocolate protein powder (Optimum Nutrition whey)	48	4	6	240
1 Tablespoon unsweetened cocoa powder	1	1	2	15
2 Tablespoons Swerve	0	0	24	0
zest of 1/4 orange	0	0	1	2
1 1/3 cups fresh orange juice (about 4 oranges)	2	0	38	159
1 teaspoon vanilla extract				
Total	**77**	**10**	**81**	**596**
Half of that big old 24 oz Deluxe container	**39**	**5**	**40**	**298**

That tiny bit of zest provides some gorgeous bitterness! Don't like bitter? Skip the zest!

1. Measure all the base ingredients into your Creami container, making sure not to pass the max fill line.
2. Blend with your immersion (stick) blender til smooth and luscious.
3. Pop into your freezer for 24 hours.
4. Pop into your Ninja Creami Deluxe. Select full, make your selection, and hit the go button.
5. Take a peek. Perfectly creamy? Great! If not, add 1-2 Tablespoons of vanilla almond milk and select full and push the re-spin button. (Usually requires a re-spin.
6. Enjoy!

Makes a 24 oz Deluxe pint. Have a smaller 16 oz model? Cut all the ingredients to 2/3.

Peaches and Cream

Ingredient	Protein	Fat	Carbs	Calories
1 cup 2% Daisy cottage cheese	26	5	10	180
2 scoops vanilla protein powder (Optimum Nutrition Whey)	48	3	8	240
2 cups frozen peaches, thawed	2	0	30	120
2 Tablespoon Swerve	0	0	24	0
1/4 teaspoon lorann super strength peach flavor				
1 teaspoon vanilla extract				
Optional: 3 drops each of red & yellow food coloring				
Total	76	8	72	540
Half of that big old 24 oz Deluxe container	38	4	36	270

If some is good, is more better? 1/4 teaspoon of the super strength peach flavor tastes like peaches. 1/2 teaspoon makes it tasted like those peach ring candies.

1. Measure all the base ingredients into your Creami container, making sure not to pass the max fill line.
2. Blend with your immersion (stick) blender til smooth and luscious.
3. Pop into your freezer for 24 hours.
4. Pop into your Ninja Creami Deluxe. Select full, make your selection, and hit the go button.
5. Take a peek. Perfectly creamy? Great! If not, add 1-2 Tablespoons of vanilla almond milk and select full and push the re-spin button. (Usually requires a re-spin.
6. Enjoy!

Natural color →
← Enhanced color

Makes a 24 oz Deluxe pint. Have a smaller 16 oz model? Cut all the ingredients to 2/3.

Peach Melba

Ingredient	Protein	Fat	Carbs	Calories
1 cup 2% Daisy cottage cheese	26	5	10	180
2 scoops vanilla protein powder (Optimum Nutrition Whey)	48	3	8	240
1 1/3 cups frozen peaches, thawed	1	0	20	80
2/3 cup frozen raspberries, thawed	1	1	11	40
1 teaspoon lemon juice	0	0	0	2
1 Tablespoon Swerve	0	0	12	0
1/4 teaspoon lorann super strength peach flavor				
1/4 teaspoon raspberry extract				
1 teaspoon vanilla extract				
Optional: a few drops of red and yellow food coloring				
Total	76	9	61	542
Half of that big old 24 oz Deluxe container	**38**	**5**	**31**	**271**

Chopped up frozen peaches and raspberries make a darling mix-in!

1. Measure all the base ingredients into your Creami container, making sure not to pass the max fill line.
2. Blend with your immersion (stick) blender til smooth and luscious.
3. Pop into your freezer for 24 hours.
4. Pop into your Ninja Creami Deluxe. Select full, make your selection, and hit the go button.
5. Take a peek. Perfectly creamy? Great! If not, add 1-2 Tablespoons of vanilla almond milk and select full and push the re-spin button. (Usually requires a re-spin.
6. Enjoy!

Makes a 24 oz Deluxe pint. Have a smaller 16 oz model? Cut all the ingredients to 2/3.

Jen's Apricot Cardamom Dreams	Protein	Fat	Carbs	Calories
1 cup 2% Daisy cottage cheese	26	5	10	180
2 scoops vanilla protein powder (Optimum Nutrition Whey)	48	3	8	240
1 can Jumex apricot nectar	0	0	38	150
1/2 teaspoon ground cardamom				
2 Tablespoons Swerve	0	0	24	0
1 teaspoon vanilla extract				
Total	74	8	80	570
Half of that big old 24 oz Deluxe container	37	4	40	285
MIX-IN! 2 Tablespoons chopped dried apricots/person	1	0	13	55
MIX-IN! 2 Tablespoons chopped pistachios/person	2	4	2	43
MIX-IN! 2 Tablespoons unsweetened coconut per person	1	7	3	70
Half plus mix-ins	40	14	57	453

1. Measure all the base ingredients (not mix-ins or toppings!) into your Creami container, making sure not to pass the max fill line.
2. Blend with your immersion (stick) blender til smooth and luscious.
3. Pop into your freezer for 24 hours.
4. Pop into your Ninja Creami Deluxe. Select full, make your selection, and hit the go button.
5. Take a peek. Perfectly creamy? Great! If not, add 1-2 Tablespoons of vanilla almond milk and select full and push the re-spin button. (Usually requires a re-spin.
6. Add in the **chopped up mix-ins** in a column up the center of the container and hit full, mix in.
7. Enjoy!

Makes a 24 oz Deluxe pint. Have a smaller 16 oz model? Cut all the ingredients to 2/3.

Pumpkin pie à la Mode

Ingredient	Protein	Fat	Carbs	Calories
1 cup 2% Daisy cottage cheese	26	5	10	180
2 scoops vanilla protein powder (Optimum Nutrition Whey)	48	3	8	240
1 1/4 c pumpkin puree *(Not pie filling!)*	3	1	25	113
3 Tablespoons Swerve - brown sugar	0	0	36	0
1/2 teaspoon ground cinnamon				
1/4 teaspoon ground ginger (Optional)				
1/4 teaspoon ground cardamom (Optional)				
small pinch ground cloves (Optional)				
small pinch ground allspice (Optional)				
1 teaspoon vanilla extract				
Total	77	9	79	533
Half of that big old 24 oz Deluxe container	38	5	40	266

optional toppings: pecans, pie crust, graham crackers, whipped cream

1. Measure all the base ingredients into your Creami container, making sure not to pass the max fill line.
2. Blend with your immersion (stick) blender til smooth and luscious.
3. Pop into your freezer for 24 hours.
4. Pop into your Ninja Creami Deluxe. Select full, make your selection, and hit the go button.
5. Take a peek. Perfectly creamy? Great! If not, add 1-2 Tablespoons of vanilla almond milk and select full and push the re-spin button. (Usually requires a re-spin.
6. Enjoy!

Makes a 24 oz Deluxe pint. Have a smaller 16 oz model? Cut all the ingredients to 2/3.

Bananas Foster

Ingredient	Protein	Fat	Carbs	Calories
1 cup 2% Daisy cottage cheese	26	5	10	180
2 scoops vanilla protein powder (Optimum Nutrition Whey)	48	3	8	240
2 bananas	3	1	54	210
3 Tablespoons brown sugar swerve	0	0	36	0
3/4 teaspoon rum extract				
1/2 teaspoon butter extract				
1/4 cup vanilla almond milk	0	1	0	8
Total	77	10	108	638
Half of that big old 24 oz Deluxe container	38	5	54	319

Opt: bananas, whipped cream, caramel

1. Measure all the base ingredients (not mix-ins or toppings!) into your Creami container, making sure not to pass the max fill line.
2. Blend with your immersion (stick) blender til smooth and luscious.
3. Pop into your freezer for 24 hours.
4. Pop into your Ninja Creami Deluxe. Select full, make your selection, and hit the go button.
5. Take a peek. Perfectly creamy? Great! If not, add 1-2 Tablespoons of vanilla almond milk and select full and push the re-spin button. (Usually requires a re-spin.
6. Enjoy!

Makes a 24 oz Deluxe pint. Have a smaller 16 oz model? Cut all the ingredients to 2/3.

Banana Chocolate Chip Walnut	Protein	Fat	Carbs	Calories
1 cup 2% Daisy cottage cheese	26	5	10	180
2 scoops vanilla protein powder (Optimum Nutrition Whey)	48	3	8	240
2 bananas	3	1	54	210
1/4 c pb fit	16	4	12	120
1 Tablespoons vanilla almond milk	0	0	0	2
Total	93	13	84	752
Half of that big old 24 oz Deluxe container	46	6	42	376
MIX-IN! 2 T walnuts per person	1	5	1	50
MIX-IN! 2 T mini chocolate chips per person	0	8	18	140
Half with 2 T walnuts and chocolate chips	47	19	61	566

The add-ins put it over the top!

1. Measure all the base ingredients (not mix-ins or toppings!) into your Creami container, making sure not to pass the max fill line.
2. Blend with your immersion (stick) blender til smooth and luscious.
3. Pop into your freezer for 24 hours.
4. Pop into your Ninja Creami Deluxe. Select full, make your selection, and hit the go button.
5. Take a peek. Perfectly creamy? Great! If not, add 1-2 Tablespoons of vanilla almond milk and select full and push the re-spin button. (Usually requires a re-spin.
6. Add in the **chopped up nuts and chips** in a column up the center of the container and hit full, mix in.
7. Enjoy!

Makes a 24 oz Deluxe pint. Have a smaller 16 oz model? Cut all the ingredients to 2/3.

Baby Guava

	Protein	Fat	Carbs	Calories
1 cup 2% Daisy cottage cheese	26	5	10	180
2 scoops vanilla protein powder (Optimum Nutrition Whey)	48	3	8	240
1 3/4 cups baby guavas, quartered	7	3	42	192
1 Tablespoon Swerve	0	0	12	0
2 Tablespoons vanilla almond milk	0	0	0	4
1 teaspoon vanilla extract				
Total	81	11	72	616
Half of that big old 24 oz Deluxe container	41	5	36	308

Baby guavas have seeds!!! Seeds are just no fun. After you blend it, you need to push the mixture through a sieve to get all those seeds out. Worth it? Oh my gosh, yes! The flavor is just as wonderful as their intoxicating fragrance. If you're below the max fill line after, just stir in a little more almond milk.

1. Measure all the base ingredients (not mix-ins or toppings!) into your Creami container, making sure not to pass the max fill line.
2. Blend with your immersion (stick) blender til smooth and luscious.
3. Pop into your freezer for 24 hours.
4. Pop into your Ninja Creami Deluxe. Select full, make your selection, and hit the go button.
5. Take a peek. Perfectly creamy? Great! If not, add 1-2 Tablespoons of vanilla almond milk and select full and push the re-spin button. (Usually requires a re-spin.
6. Enjoy!

**Using nutrition info for regular guava. Numbers on baby guava just aren't out there.

Makes a 24 oz Deluxe pint. Have a smaller 16 oz model? Cut all the ingredients to 2/3.

Chocolate Cherry

Ingredient	Protein	Fat	Carbs	Calories
1 cup 2% Daisy cottage cheese	26	5	10	180
2 scoops chocolate protein powder (Optimum Nutrition whey)	48	4	6	240
1 1/2 cups frozen cherries, thawed	2	0	33	135
1 Tablespoon unsweetened cocoa powder	1	1	2	15
2 Tablespoons Swerve	0	0	24	0
1 teaspoon almond extract				
total	77	10	75	570
Half of that big old 24 oz Deluxe container	**38**	**5**	**38**	**285**

Measure frozen fruit while it's frozen!!!

1. Measure all the base ingredients (not mix-ins or toppings!) into your Creami container, making sure not to pass the max fill line.
2. Blend with your immersion (stick) blender til smooth and luscious.
3. Pop into your freezer for 24 hours.
4. Pop into your Ninja Creami Deluxe. Select full, make your selection, and hit the go button.
5. Take a peek. Perfectly creamy? Great! If not, add 1-2 Tablespoons of vanilla almond milk and select full and push the re-spin button. (Usually requires a re-spin.
6. Enjoy!

Tastes just like chocolate covered cherries!

Makes a 24 oz Deluxe pint. Have a smaller 16 oz model? Cut all the ingredients to 2/3.

Cookies and Cream

	Protein	Fat	Carbs	Calories
1 cup 2% Daisy cottage cheese	26	5	10	180
1 scoop chocolate protein powder (Optimum Nutrition whey)	24	2	3	120
1 scoop vanilla protein powder (Optimum Nutrition whey)	24	2	4	120
1 1/4 c chocolate almond milk (to line)	1	3	24	125
Total	75	12	41	545
Half of that big old 24 oz Deluxe container	**38**	**6**	**20**	**273**
MIX-IN! 4 Oreo thins per person	1	6	21	140
Half with 4 cookies	**39**	**12**	**41**	**413**

Half with 4 cookies and a little extra cream..

1/4 cup extra creamy Reddi wip	0	2	0	30
Half with 4 cookies and a little extra cream..	**39**	**14**	**41**	**443**

The cookies are 8/10 recommended, but the whipped cream is truly optional.

1. Measure all the base ingredients (not mix-ins or toppings!) into your Creami container, making sure not to pass the max fill line.
2. Blend with your immersion (stick) blender til smooth and luscious.
3. Pop into your freezer for 24 hours.
4. Pop into your Ninja Creami Deluxe. Select full, make your selection, and hit the go button.
5. Take a peek. Perfectly creamy? Great! If not, add 1-2 Tablespoons of vanilla almond milk and select full and push the re-spin button. (Usually requires a re-spin.
6. Add in the **chopped up cookies** in a column up the center of the container and hit full, mix in.
7. Enjoy!

Makes a 24 oz Deluxe pint. Have a smaller 16 oz model? Cut all the ingredients to 2/3.

Chocolate Malt

Ingredient	Protein	Fat	Carbs	Calories
1 cup 2% Daisy cottage cheese	26	5	10	180
2 scoops chocolate protein powder (Optimum Nutrition whey)	48	4	6	240
1/4 c malt powder	3	2	21	120
1 Tablespoon unsweetened cocoa powder	1	1	2	15
2 Tablespoons Swerve	0	0	24	0
1 c chocolate almond milk	1	2	19	100
Total	79	14	82	655
Half of that big old 24 oz Deluxe container	39	7	41	327
MIX-IN! 10 whoppers per person	0	4	18	108
half plus 10 whoppers	39	11	59	435

Candy totally optional! The base is filled with chocolate malt flavor!

1. Measure all the base ingredients (not mix-ins or toppings!) into your Creami container, making sure not to pass the max fill line.
2. Blend with your immersion (stick) blender til smooth and luscious.
3. Pop into your freezer for 24 hours.
4. Pop into your Ninja Creami Deluxe. Select full, make your selection, and hit the go button.
5. Take a peek. Perfectly creamy? Great! If not, add 1-2 Tablespoons of vanilla almond milk and select full and push the re-spin button. (Usually requires a re-spin.
6. Add in the **chopped up candy** in a column up the center of the container and hit full, mix in.
7. Enjoy!

Makes a 24 oz Deluxe pint. Have a smaller 16 oz model? Cut all the ingredients to 2/3.

Chocolate Peanut Butter

	Protein	Fat	Carbs	Calories
1 cup 2% Daisy cottage cheese	26	5	10	180
2 scoops chocolate protein powder (Optimum Nutrition whey)	48	4	6	240
6 Tablespoons PB fit	24	6	18	180
1 Tablespoon unsweetened cocoa powder	1	1	2	15
2 Tablespoons Swerve	0	0	24	0
1 c chocolate almond milk (to line)	1	2	19	100
Total	100	18	79	715
Half of that big old 24 oz Deluxe container	50	9	40	358
MIX-IN! 3 mini regular peanut butter cups/person	3	7	15	130
half plus 3 mini pb cups	53	16	55	488

The candy is totally optional! The base has all the flavor!

1. Measure all the base ingredients (not mix-ins or toppings!) into your Creami container, making sure not to pass the max fill line.
2. Blend with your immersion (stick) blender til smooth and luscious.
3. Pop into your freezer for 24 hours.
4. Pop into your Ninja Creami Deluxe. Select full, make your selection, and hit the go button.
5. Take a peek. Perfectly creamy? Great! If not, add 1-2 Tablespoons of vanilla almond milk and select full and push the re-spin button. (Usually requires a re-spin.
6. Add in the **chopped up candy** in a column up the center of the container and hit full, mix in.
7. Enjoy!

Makes a 24 oz Deluxe pint. Have a smaller 16 oz model? Cut all the ingredients to 2/3.

Red Velvet

Ingredient	Protein	Fat	Carbs	Calories
1 cup 2% Daisy cottage cheese	26	5	10	180
2 scoops chocolate protein powder (Optimum Nutrition whey)	48	4	6	240
1 Tablespoon unsweetened cocoa powder	1	1	2	15
1/4 cup low fat buttermilk (Oak farms)	2	1	4	30
1/2 teaspoon white vinegar	0	0	0	1
1 oz low fat Philadelphia cream cheese	2	6	0	70
2 Tablespoons Swerve - powdered sugar	0	0	24	0
1 teaspoon vanilla extract				
3/4 c chocolate almond milk to line	1	2	14	75
2 teaspoons red food coloring (Optional!!)				
total	80	19	60	611
Half of that big old 24 oz Deluxe container	**40**	**9**	**30**	**305**

Don't want to use food coloring? Totally okay! Call it retro! Originally, it was called Red Velvet Cake for the slightly red color that occurred naturally from the ingredients. Red food coloring and cream cheese frosting came later!

1. Measure all the base ingredients (not mix-ins or toppings!) into your Creami container, making sure not to pass the max fill line.
2. Blend with your immersion (stick) blender til smooth and luscious.
3. Pop into your freezer for 24 hours.
4. Pop into your Ninja Creami Deluxe. Select full, make your selection, and hit the go button.
5. Take a peek. Perfectly creamy? Great! If not, add 1-2 Tablespoons of vanilla almond milk and select full and push the re-spin button. (Usually requires a re-spin.
6. Enjoy!

Makes a 24 oz Deluxe pint. Have a smaller 16 oz model? Cut all the ingredients to 2/3.

S'mores

	Protein	Fat	Carbs	Calories
1 cup 2% Daisy cottage cheese	26	5	10	180
2 scoops smores protein powder (Optimum Nutrition whey)	48	4	6	260
1 Tablespoon unsweetened cocoa powder	1	1	2	15
2 Tablespoons Swerve	0	0	24	0
1 1/4 c chocolate almond milk (to line)	1	3	24	125
Total	76	13	66	580
Half of that big old 24 oz Deluxe container	**38**	**7**	**33**	**290**
MIX-IN! 1 T mini chocolate chips/person	0	4	9	70
MIX-IN! 1 graham cracker sheet/person	1	2	12	65
MIX-IN! 2 max mallow marshmallows/person	1	0	5	15
half plus mix ins	**40**	**12**	**59**	**440**

1. Measure all the base ingredients (not mix-ins or toppings!) into your Creami container, making sure not to pass the max fill line.
2. Blend with your immersion (stick) blender til smooth and luscious.
3. Pop into your freezer for 24 hours.
4. Pop into your Ninja Creami Deluxe. Select full, make your selection, and hit the go button.
5. Take a peek. Perfectly creamy? Great! If not, add 1-2 Tablespoons of vanilla almond milk and select full and push the re-spin button. (Usually requires a re-spin.
6. Add in the **chopped up mix-ins** in a column up the center of the container and hit full, mix in.
7. Enjoy!

Makes a 24 oz Deluxe pint. Have a smaller 16 oz model? Cut all the ingredients to 2/3.

Pistachio

	Protein	Fat	Carbs	Calories
1 cup 2% Daisy cottage cheese	26	5	10	180
2 scoops vanilla protein powder (Optimum Nutrition Whey)	48	3	8	240
1/2 cup pistachios	6	14	8	170
1 c vanilla almond milk	1	3	1	30
1 T Swerve	0	0	12	0
1 teaspoon almond extract				
Total	81	25	39	620
Half of that big old 24 oz Deluxe container	41	12	20	310
MIX-IN! 1/4 c pistachios added in per person	3	7	4	85
Half plus 1/4 c pistachios	44	19	24	395

You could add a few drops of green food coloring, but I love the natural pistachio color...

1. Measure all the base ingredients (not mix-ins or toppings!) into your Creami container, making sure not to pass the max fill line.
2. Blend with your immersion (stick) blender til smooth and luscious.
3. Pop into your freezer for 24 hours.
4. Pop into your Ninja Creami Deluxe. Select full, make your selection, and hit the go button.
5. Take a peek. Perfectly creamy? Great! If not, add 1-2 Tablespoons of vanilla almond milk and select full and push the re-spin button. (Usually requires a re-spin.
6. Add in the **chopped up pistachios** in a column up the center of the container and hit full, mix in.
7. Enjoy!

If your pistachios are salted, be sure to give them a rinse and pat dry!

Makes a 24 oz Deluxe pint. Have a smaller 16 oz model? Cut all the ingredients

King Cake

	Protein	Fat	Carbs	Calories
1 cup 2% Daisy cottage cheese	26	5	10	180
2 scoops vanilla protein powder (Optimum Nutrition Whey)	48	3	8	240
1/4 c swerve	0	0	48	0
1/2 teaspoon ground cinnamon				
pinch ground nutmeg				
zest half lemon	0	0	1	2
1 1/4 c Vanilla almond milk	1	3	1	38
Total	75	11	68	459
Half of that big old 24 oz Deluxe container	38	6	34	230

Optional, but obviously vital! wee plastic baby doll, purple, yellow, and green sprinkles

1. Measure all the base ingredients (not mix-ins or toppings!) into your Creami container, making sure not to pass the max fill line.
2. Blend with your immersion (stick) blender til smooth and luscious.
3. Pop into your freezer for 24 hours.
4. Pop into your Ninja Creami Deluxe. Select full, make your selection, and hit the go button.
5. Take a peek. Perfectly creamy? Great! If not, add 1-2 Tablespoons of vanilla almond milk and select full and push the re-spin button. (Usually requires a re-spin.
6. Enjoy!

Makes a 24 oz Deluxe pint. Have a smaller 16 oz model? Cut all the ingredients to 2/3.

Churro

Ingredients	Protein	Fat	Carbs	Calories
1 cup 2% Daisy cottage cheese	26	5	10	180
2 scoops vanilla protein powder (Optimum Nutrition Whey)	48	3	8	240
3 Tablespoons Swerve - brown sugar	0	0	36	0
3/4 teaspoon ground cinnamon				
1 1/2 teaspoons Lorann buttery sweet dough extract				
1 1/4 cup vanilla almond milk	1	3	1	38
Total	75	11	55	458
Half of that big old 24 oz Deluxe container	**38**	**6**	**28**	**229**

optional toppings: A churro or Siete churro chip pieces

1. Measure all the base ingredients (not mix-ins or toppings!) into your Creami container, making sure not to pass the max fill line.
2. Blend with your immersion (stick) blender til smooth and luscious.
3. Pop into your freezer for 24 hours.
4. Pop into your Ninja Creami Deluxe. Select full, make your selection, and hit the go button.
5. Take a peek. Perfectly creamy? Great! If not, add 1-2 Tablespoons of vanilla almond milk and select full and push the re-spin button. (Usually requires a re-spin.
6. Enjoy!

Makes a 24 oz Deluxe pint. Have a smaller 16 oz model? Cut all the ingredients to 2/3.

Cookie Dough

	Protein	Fat	Carbs	Calories
1 cup 2% Daisy cottage cheese	26	5	10	180
2 scoops vanilla protein powder (Optimum Nutrition Whey)	48	3	8	240
1 1/4 c vanilla almond milk	1	3	1	38
1 teaspoon vanilla extract				
Total	75	11	19	458
Half of that big old 24 oz Deluxe container	**38**	**6**	**10**	**229**
MIX-IN! **7 cookie dough balls per person**	1	10	20	148
half with 7 cookie dough balls	**39**	**16**	**30**	**376**

The cookie dough balls are the flavor. Totally necessary!

1. Measure all the base ingredients (not mix-ins or toppings!) into your Creami container, making sure not to pass the max fill line.
2. Blend with your immersion (stick) blender til smooth and luscious.
3. Pop into your freezer for 24 hours.
4. Pop into your Ninja Creami Deluxe. Select full, make your selection, and hit the go button.
5. Take a peek. Perfectly creamy? Great! If not, add 1-2 Tablespoons of vanilla almond milk and select full and push the re-spin button. (Usually requires a re-spin.
6. Add in the **chopped up cookie dough** in a column up the center of the container and hit full, mix in.
7. Enjoy!

Makes a 24 oz Deluxe pint. Have a smaller 16 oz model? Cut all the ingredients to 2/3.

Cookie Dough to add in (56 balls)

	Protein	Fat	Carbs	Calories
1/4 c butter	0	44	0	400
2T swerve	0	0	24	0
2T brown sugar swerve	0	0	24	0
1/2 t vanilla extract				
1/2 c oat flour	8	4	40	220
1/4 t salt				
1/2 c mini chocolate chips	0	32	72	560
Total	8	80	160	1180
(14 balls) quarter	2	20	40	295
(7 balls) eighth	1	10	20	148

Mix all the ingredients together.

Roll into 56 balls.

Place them on a parchment covered baking sheet in the freezer.

Freeze overnight.

The next morning, put thrm all in a Ziploc freezer bag and put them back in the freezer.

Every time you make a 24 ounce batch of cookie dough nice cream for two people, you'll add 14 chopped up cookie balls. (7 per person.)

Thin Mint

	Protein	Fat	Carbs	Calories
1 cup 2% Daisy cottage cheese	26	5	10	180
2 scoops Thin Mint protein powder (GNC Wheybolic)	40	2	8	200
1 1/4 c Chocolate almond milk (to line)	1	3	24	125
Total	67	10	42	505
Half of that big old 24 oz Deluxe container	34	5	21	253
MIX-IN! 4 cookies per person	1	7	22	160
Half plus 4 cookies per person	35	12	43	413

The cookies are 8/10 recommended!

1. Measure all the base ingredients (not mix-ins or toppings!) into your Creami container, making sure not to pass the max fill line.
2. Blend with your immersion (stick) blender til smooth and luscious.
3. Pop into your freezer for 24 hours.
4. Pop into your Ninja Creami Deluxe. Select full, make your selection, and hit the go button.
5. Take a peek. Perfectly creamy? Great! If not, add 1-2 Tablespoons of vanilla almond milk and select full and push the re-spin button. (Usually requires a re-spin.
6. Add in the **chopped up cookies** in a column up the center of the container and hit full, mix in.
7. Enjoy!

Makes a 24 oz Deluxe pint. Have a smaller 16 oz model? Cut all the ingredients to 2/3.

Caramel DeLite

	Protein	Fat	Carbs	Calories
1 cup 2% Daisy cottage cheese	26	5	10	180
2 scoops caramel delite protein powder	40	2	8	200
1 1/4 c Thai kitchen light coconut milk	0	19	8	188
total	66	25	26	568
Half of that big old 24 oz Deluxe container	33	13	13	284
MIX-IN! 2 cookies per person	0	6	19	140
Half plus 2 cookies per person	33	19	32	424

Opt: whipped cream, coconut, chocolate chips, caramel or chocolate drizzle

The cookies are 8/10 recommended!

1. Measure all the base ingredients (not mix-ins or toppings!) into your Creami container, making sure not to pass the max fill line.
2. Blend with your immersion (stick) blender til smooth and luscious.
3. Pop into your freezer for 24 hours.
4. Pop into your Ninja Creami Deluxe. Select full, make your selection, and hit the go button.
5. Take a peek. Perfectly creamy? Great! If not, add 1-2 Tablespoons of vanilla almond milk and select full and push the re-spin button. (Usually requires a re-spin.
6. Add in the **chopped up cookies** in a column up the center of the container and hit full, mix in.
7. Enjoy!

Makes a 24 oz Deluxe pint. Have a smaller 16 oz model? Cut all the ingredients to 2/3.

40

Biscoff

	Protein	Fat	Carbs	Calories
1 cup 2% Daisy cottage cheese	26	5	10	180
2 scoops vanilla protein powder (Optimum Nutrition Whey)	48	3	8	240
2 T Biscoff butter	1	11	17	170
1 1/4 c vanilla almond milk	1	3	1	38
1 teaspoon vanilla extract				
Total	76	22	36	628
Half of that big old 24 oz Deluxe container	**38**	**11**	**18**	**314**
MIX-IN! 4 cookies per person	2	6	23	150
Half plus 4 cookies	**40**	**17**	**41**	**464**

Loaded Biscoff - Half plus whipped cream and a caramel drizzle...

	Protein	Fat	Carbs	Calories
1/4 cup Extra Creamy Reddi Wip	0	2	0	30
2 T Jordan's Skinny Sauces Salted Caramel	0	0	0	0
Loaded Biscoff total	**40**	**19**	**41**	**494**

The cookies are totally necessary to the flavor!

The whipped cream and caramel syrup are optional.

1. Measure all the base ingredients (not mix-ins or toppings!) into your Creami container, making sure not to pass the max fill line.
2. Blend with your immersion (stick) blender til smooth and luscious.
3. Pop into your freezer for 24 hours.
4. Pop into your Ninja Creami Deluxe. Select full, make your selection, and hit the go button.
5. Take a peek. Perfectly creamy? Great! If not, add 1-2 Tablespoons of vanilla almond milk and select full and push the re-spin button. (Usually requires a re-spin.)
6. Add in the **chopped up cookies** in a column up the center of the container and hit full, mix in.
7. Enjoy!

Makes a 24 oz Deluxe pint. Have a smaller 16 oz model? Cut all the ingredients to 2/3.

Just leaving this little vegetable sculpture here that I did a few years back because he always gets people's attention. :D Thanks again for buying my book! I hope you love it! Please leave a review on Amazon if you're so inclined!

xx Jen

Jennifer Guerrero
the not so starving artist

Love this? Come find my blog! I'm a food blogger and cookbook reviewer! So many delicious recipes to try! No clickbait anywhere and no "jump to recipe" because there's no fluff. Just recipes with Amazon affiliate links for some of my kitchen favorites *after* the recipes.

The Not So Starving Artist

www.JenniferGuerrero.com

Instagram @starvingartisteats

Check out my other books!

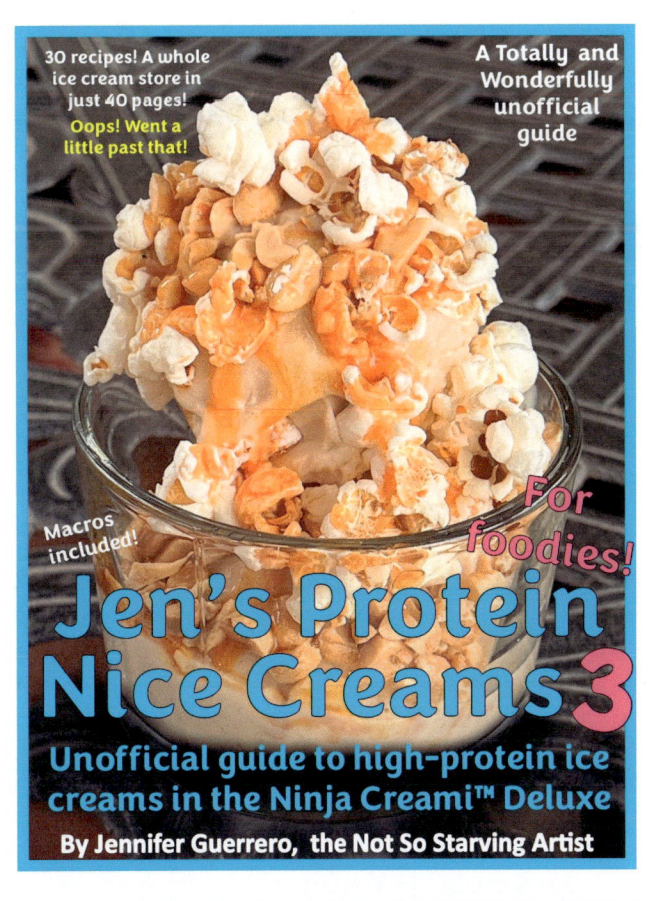

Made in United States
Troutdale, OR
06/02/2024

20259788R00026